BETWEEN THE SLATES
and
TAILS FROM
"The Happy Hunting Ground"

Between the Slates

and

TAILS FROM

"The Happy Hunting Ground"

By
ANNA LOUISE FLETCHER

WASHINGTON, D. C.
MCMXXXIV

CONTENTS

PART I
                                         PAGE
BETWEEN THE SLATES 9

PART II
FURTHER CORROBORATIVE EVIDENCE 25

PART III
TAILS FROM "THE HAPPY HUNTING GROUND" 39

PART I
BETWEEN THE SLATES

PART I

BETWEEN THE SLATES

During the summer of 1925, I was privileged to have a sitting with Pierre Keeler. All doors and windows were open in the room where the sitting was held. I had written the names on a piece of paper, the night before, of those in the Spirit World I wished to contact. I carried it to Mr. Keeler's residence in my handbag, folded closely with the writing inside. He asked how many I was seeking, and placed that number of cards, with a bit of pencil lead, between two slates, put a rubber strap around to keep them solid, and my crumpled paper on top, in plain view every minute. He had no chance to read what I had written, for we spent the time, waiting for the signal, in conversation. I was much interested in hearing him tell of a proposition which Houdini had made to him for a test. He had arrived at the entrance to the Lily Dale Assembly grounds, evidently fearing to enter, and had requested, by messenger, an audience with Mr. Keeler; which took place at the gate, Houdini proposing that Mr. Keeler should give him a sitting, but in the presence of a Catholic priest. The noted medium was not caught in that trap!

I have seen Houdini give a demonstration of his version of obtaining slate writing, and it was a silly performance. He had an accomplice sitting at his side, and the slates he held were passed, with magicianship rapidity, under the table, and exchanged for some containing writing. Even Houdini's sleight of hand did not hide the trick. The messages were not from loved ones of the witnesses, but from noted personages.

There are some doubters of psychic phenomena who think that Mr. Keeler must, in some superhuman way, manipulate the writing on those cards, but I am absolutely sure that there was not the slightest chance during that first sitting nor in any subsequent ones. As soon as Mr. Keeler's account of his encounter with Houdini was ended, the signal came to hold the slates. He held one side, I the other, with the slates about a foot from the top of the table. The writing was heard and felt, the process took about five minutes, and all cards were covered with writing.

I had written on my paper: "Mary Minton Paine—can you tell me anything about the portrait?"

Because an oil painting of her had disappeared in the great Jacksonville fire of 1901, and Mrs. Hughes, Baltimore medium, once said to me, without any suggestion on my part, or knowledge of that picture: "That picture went by way of water, and not by fire."

In her answer on one of the cards, the writing is of very fine type, contains two lines of a poem, and 106 words, and is signed:

"I am with love *grandma*
"Mary Minton Paine."

There was not, by the most preposterous surmising, any chance for the medium to know that "Mary Minton Paine" was my "grandmother." She passed out of mortal life when I was about ten years old. In the corner of her card is a penciled head, apparently drawn under the writing. A cousin, who had been an amateur artist, told me in a sitting with a trance medium that she had attempted to draw William James, and it is not unlike some of his pictures. At that time, I had never seen a specimen of my grandmother's mortal writing, but it was verified later as corresponding with that on the card.

In giving the description of this card and others to follow, I am using the capitals, punctuations, etc., as they appear on the cards.

The summer of 1926 I was again in Lily Dale and had a sitting with Mr. Keeler. Though I received several personal messages, I had gone to him especially to obtain messages for people I did not know, who had written, begging me to intercede for them. Those I mailed to the people requesting them. I had a strong suspicion that one especially had come from a Houdini spy, as I had been warned through Hazel Ridley, by a Spirit Lawyer, "to watch out for tricks!" What a plum it would have been for Houdini to be able to discredit Keeler through me! He had been on the war-path against all mediums, and he also did not have any kindly feeling for me, after I gave my testimony before the committee hearings on "The Houdini Fortune Telling Bill."

The answer to the request under suspicion was dictated by the Spirit Lawyer who had warned me, and was legally clever. It could not have given offense, had the object been true, but must have given a surprise, if the whole affair was a fake. I never received any acknowledgment from the young woman to whom it was sent, thereby rather strengthening my suspicion.

During the summer of 1927 it was impossible for me to visit Lily Dale, so I commissioned my friend, Miss Belle Cross, to have a sitting for me with Mr. Keeler. The names of my spirit friends were written by me in Washington, placed in an envelope, sealed, and mailed in a letter to Miss Cross, and she has assured me that she broke the seal after the writing of the cards was finished, and only then did she become aware of its contents. All friends designated answered, and there were three messages from personalities not included, among them one from my grandmother. She began with, "Dear Lulu Fletcher." "Lulu" was the nickname which she had given me, and I had not used for several years. The medium could not have had any mortal way of knowing I had been called by that name. There were 136 words in that message, two lines of poetry, and the writing identical with that of 1925. Miss Cross timed the writing of the cards, and there were 423 words written in 2 minutes and 40 seconds.

In the spring of 1933 I had a sitting with Mr. Keeler in Washington. I had written at home seven names of friends in the Spirit World and received answers from five, although I had heard previously from the silent ones through trumpet and trance mediums. In addition to the five messages, there were *six others not* included in my appeal, notably one again from my grandmother, the writing identical with the two former specimens. This third card is, like the others, so remarkable that I feel I must quote it in full:

"Dearest Anna Louise:

"When I see any one with natural freedom curtailed, I feel sorry that I cannot replenish the larder of joys and freedom which so abounded in the early springtime of life. Yet as I look at this condition and that, I always find a solace in the conclusion that the situation of any loved one of mine, is never so bad, but it could be worse. Hence after all there is a Thanksgiving Day for one and all. Jean Ingelow aptly expressed it in her song of 'Regret':

" 'When I remember something which I had,
But which is gone and I must do without,
I sometimes wonder how I can be glad,
Even in cowslip time when hedges sprout;

It makes we sigh to think on it—but yet
My days will not be better days, should I forget.'
"With tender regard grandma
"Mary Minton Paine."

The message is very significant owing to my accident and subsequent lameness. There are not any omissions in punctuation nor lettering, and the style of writing duplicates the previous cards.

In the corner of this card is a drawn head, apparently under the writing, as before, and represents George Christy, the medium's guide. My artist cousin must have been with grandmother, and doing her part.

Among the cards of that sitting was a message from a man I had never known. I had met casually his sister-in-law, and knew that her sister had lost her husband, and that the name was "Brown." This message contains his given name, a short but pertinent message and, his relatives have told me, in his handwriting. The name Brown was not in my mind nor on my paper, and a communication from him was as improbable as any I can think of. Only an intense desire to send a message to those he loved could have directed this effort through mental channels of ignorance in regard to him.

During the spring of 1934 I again had a sitting with Mr. Keeler in Washington. Not fearing any failure, I determined to make a fraud proof test. I wrote on a sheet of paper, six names. Then I folded it, and pasted the edges firmly together. I folded it again into a small bundle, and tied it with heavy thread. The medium made no comment nor objection to this. The cards and slates were fixed as usual, and my folded and tied paper placed on top. It must be remembered that the table, slates, sitters and Mr. Keeler are located by a window in broad daylight. Only a person steeped in suspicion could be deceived by any supposed surreptitious movements.

After a few moments' conversation, the slates were picked up, the writing heard and felt, and in less time than it takes to write it, my paper was placed on the table, the elastic band removed, the two slates separated, and Mr. Keeler threw out the filled cards, remarking, "Why, there is a picture of a dog on that top card." I said, "I wrote something about a cat," but as I said this he was picking up some blank cards, which had been lying on the window sill, slipped the thread from my pasted and folded paper, so it could be placed flat on top of the cards between the slates, where there is very little room, and we were again holding them, the writing was again heard and felt, and this had been done without the slightest delay, Mr. Keeler remarking, "My Guide told me to try again." This medium very often receives clairaudient messages from his Guide, as the work progresses.

In about two minutes the writing was accomplished, the slates separated, and on top of the cards was my paper, torn to bits! The medium quietly remarked, without any apparent resentment: "My Guide says he did not like the way you fixed your paper." On those cards, of both groups, there were messages from the six called for, and six not called for. Among those *not* named, again in her now well known handwriting, was a message from my grandmother.

"Dear Anna Louise:

"I shall feel happier—for happiness is on this side marked in degrees as on earth—for having been here and communicated even hurriedly. All the previous meetings help to maintain a rapport between us, and this likewise enables us to be of help to you in your material affairs. With love
"Mary Minton Paine."

This snapshot has been kept for years in a kodak album, on a closet shelf. The medium could not have known of it nor of the dog.

"Photograph of Charles Andress' card, as it came from between the slates. His name was not on my sealed list."

This was written diagonally across one corner of the card, and on the other corner was a message from the late medium Hazel Ridley, whose name I had *not* included in my list, as I knew her dear friend, Miss Mooney, was waiting for a sitting, and I desired not to deplete any of the power. In her message I discern my grandmother's helping hand.

"Dear Mrs Fletcher,
"I have entered this wonderful abode of which the poet Whittier wrote:—
" 'Invisible and silent stands
The temple never made with hands.'
"I have found the spirit world very much as my guides had taught me I should. I have not outgrown my gratefulness to you for the kind attentions you gave me. I hope no one will feel I lost anything by coming over young. The joys I am denied on earth, are granted doubly in heaven.
"Hazel Ridley."

These two messages were written on a card 5 x 7 inches, the size of all the Keeler cards.

Perhaps the most remarkable card I have ever received is the one which I shall now describe.

"Well, well, this is great now isn't it? You see I did not come alone, I have the old friend with me. I wish you could have that quickened vision this moment, to enable you to look in upon the scene on this side of the veil. You could never again wish back to the mortal plane any one over here.
"I am
"Charles Andress."

In the corner of the card is a sketch of the dog, which he gave us years ago. I did *not* have his name in my list.

Among the faithful friends who have many times been present to encourage me is William James, thereby proving what he communicated to a British medium: "We shall make every possible use of the people, through whom we can reach your world."

It was he who came to me during my first sitting with the late Hazel Ridley, trance medium (whose mediumship was of the most unusual and remarkable type, the spirits, without any motion of the vocal cords, using her organism to project their voices), in 1924, and suggested I should write a book of my experiences. He came in 1926 in a circle with a trumpet medium, who was a stranger in Washington, and suggested the name for my book. In 1926 he wrote through Mr. Keeler that he was not yet ready to give me a foreword for my book, which I had requested. That same summer he came in company with my father, in a trumpet séance with William Cartheuser, in Lily Dale. After my father finished speaking, William James spoke, and before he left said: "In one minute you will hear the clock strike four." We had entered the séance room at two o'clock, and in a perfectly dark room all sense of time vanishes. One of the sitters counted sixty, and at that moment a clock in the next room struck "four."

In the fall of 1926 he materialized in a séance held under test-conditions in my home, standing before me, and as I looked into a pair of blue eyes, distinctly said, "Write it." A more detailed account will be found in my book, *Death Unveiled*.

In 1927, among the three who came unbidden to Miss Cross, when she was sitting for me with Mr. Keeler in Lily Dale, was the faithful friend again. Miss Cross wrote after the experience: "Wasn't it a glorious show-up? Professor James' personal message to me has me all swelled up! Some people will have to cling to the life line of Telepathy from long range, to explain all this!"

In 1929 he spoke through Miss Ridley, and dictated the foreword for my book, correcting me when I misunderstood *his word "collaborative"* for *corroborative*. A distinction of a scholar.

On New Year's Eve, a few hours before 1930 became only a memory, William James came to a circle being held with Miss Ridley, telling me he had "dropped in," as it were, to a party in London, England—had seen my daughter —told me where she was sitting in a certain room, and described the person to whom she was talking—all of which my daughter verified later.

About the same time he came in a private sitting with Miss Ridley, and gave me some very interesting information in regard to the manner in which my book had been printed.

Over the period of years in which William James has communicated in writing, the script has always been the same, likewise the signature.

He came again, among the six *not* called for during my pasted paper sitting with Mr. Keeler in 1934, and I feel sure wrote the following message to encourage me in this present effort, which I had not contemplated until then.

"Dear Mrs. Fletcher

"I did not find my interest at all lessened by perusing and reperusing 'Death Unveiled.' The saying is that one is never too old to learn something. One who carefully reads a good book will constantly be surprised with new thought thereby. Truly, without any purpose of undue congratulation, I regard your work as one of the modern classics in the literature of Spiritualism, and like the monuments that rise to people after they have left the mortal body, so will your printed words be a great monument to the inspiration which you have received.

"WILLIAM JAMES."

The twelve messages received in my 1934 sitting contained 447 words, in twelve different styles of handwriting. My tied and pasted paper proved quite a success, even if the Guide "didn't like it!"

I cannot believe that Mr. Keeler has a supernormal memory, which can register over a period of years, the writing, the modes of expression, and to fit the right names to the proper sitters, while doing this work for a great variety of persons constantly.

Mr. Keeler once told me that he had no more idea than I, how this work was accomplished, but since the advent of the radio his Guide had told him, "the process was similar."

I quote from the statements of two scientists made several years ago.

"Facsimile transmission has come. It sends a five-by-seven plate, with anything you want to put on it, a portrait, a written page, a map or a dress design. Instead of 20 words a minute, high speed radio transmission gives us 200 words a minute.

"MAJOR GENERAL GEORGE S. GIBBS."

"Development of a new communication system, designed to make possible the transmission of hundreds of different messages, simultaneously over one wave band.

"ALBERT B. CLARK, Boston."

In the spring of 1934 a friend visited me, who had received messages through Mr. Keeler, but remained a bit skeptical. I suggested that she should make a test. I would write names on a piece of tinted paper, not allowing her to know what was written—she should have a sitting with Mr. Keeler and keep her eyes fastened on that bit of blue paper every minute.

The proposed sitting took place. She put the folded paper in front of her on the table, and the medium would have been obliged to reach over to touch it, *which he did not do*. The cards, lead, slates and rubber were fixed, and my blue paper with its water lines, placed on top. While waiting for the signal, she noticed that Mr. Keeler was writing something in his lap. "Ah! ha!" she thought, "now I have caught him writing!" But he very openly folded a bit of white paper, and placed it on top of the blue paper. "Now," said my friend to herself, "my Sherlock Holmes business doesn't seem to click, for there rests that selfsame blue paper." So she said, "Mr. Keeler, I had only one piece of paper, and I see two under the strap." "I wrote something to my Guide," he answered, and obligingly removed his bit of paper, and allowed her to read: "George Christy, please come and help." What can we know of the exigencies of the Spirit World until we get there?

Very soon Mr. Keeler said, "My Guide tells me I do not need that message, for the lady herself has written to him." I had written at the end of my paper, "George Christy—Guide—I thank you for the many wonderful messages you have brought to me."

My six friends, named on the paper, all communicated, but the most important and evidential was the one from Sir Arthur Conan Doyle.

During Sir Arthur's mortal life I had considerable correspondence with him. In one of my letters I had complained of his quoting in one of his articles, a slur which Houdini had made about Keeler, and his answer I had never shown to any one.

"My dear Mrs. Fletcher

"I was very glad to hear about Keeler. I had no details before and took no side, but simply stated Houdini's claim. My attack on Houdini may have seemed to you gentle, but I think it has been the more deadly as any sign of bitterness would have weakened it.

"Yours sincerely
"A. Conan Doyle."

Utilizing the trial of the blue paper, I had written: "Sir Arthur Conan Doyle—You now know that I was right about Mr. Keeler." His answer rings true, and is permeated with the beauty of his great soul.

"To dear Mrs. Fletcher

"God bless and help you. You were entirely right about Mr. Keeler. I had no right to criticise him for I had never seen him work. I was only a mortal man and not infallible.

"Arthur Conan Doyle."

Note that "criticise" is spelled British fashion, using s instead of z.

Without making any effort to reach her friends, my skeptical guest returned with four beautiful personal messages—and chastened!

It is supposed that George Christy acts as Scout, to search the Heavenly Realms, to corral the favored ones, and bring them into communication with their Earth friends, probably by telepathy, as we are told that they live in a world governed by thought. I have wondered if it would not be easier for the Guide, if the sitters would name verbally the ones they desire to attract—but that of course would not be *"trying* the spirits," nor the medium.

I could mention a number of friends who have communicated repeatedly by way of Mr. Keeler's human radio system, using their normal writing and signatures, but I believe it was Sir Oliver Lodge who said, "One conclusive case, in psychic research, is enough to establish the fact." I feel that my grandmother's persistent efforts to reach me should pass as "one conclusive case."

I do not believe that Mr. Keeler, nor any other medium, is clever enough to accomplish these seeming miracles unaided by some higher power, but I have not written of these very personal experiences entirely with the idea of vindicating him in the minds of those who may look upon this work with suspicion—but to try to do my small bit to convince the sorrowing that, at times, under proper conditions, the Heavens are opened and we receive indisputable proof that our loved ones still live. Verily, "there are more things in heaven and earth, than ever dreamt of in (y)our philosophy."

Any one who receives a priceless gift and does not share it with his fellow men, is not worthy of the gift, and I vouch for the truth thereof, of these experiences as they came to me.

PART II

FURTHER CORROBORATIVE EVIDENCE

Lincoln Hotel,
Cincinnati, Ohio.
November 12, 1934.

Mrs. Anna Louise Fletcher,
2101 Connecticut Ave.,
Washington, D. C.

Dear Mrs. Fletcher:

A few years ago whilst, being Vice-President of the Cincinnati Psychic Research Society, I became interested in the mediumship of Mr. P. L. O. Keeler, and determined to find out for myself whether the attacks on his mediumship were warranted.

I therefore made it my business to have sittings with Mr. Keeler at several cities where he was attending Spiritualistic conventions, and also at Lily Dale, N. Y. I failed to find any evidence of trickery on his part, although I had the advantage of many criticisms of his mediumship, and especially the criticisms of the late Dr. Walter F. Prince, who as Research Officer of the American S. P. R., caused to be published a Volume of "proceedings" of that Society devoted entirely to the Keeler mediumship the gist of which was that the writing on all the cards obtained through this medium proved that they emanated from himself (Keeler), and these criticisms were made although Dr. Prince admitted that he had not had a single sitting with this medium.

Being satisfied that there was no fraud in such sittings, though possibly the writing did partake somewhat of the characteristics of Mr. Keeler, caused in some way at present unknown, through the mere fact that they came through his organism, I decided to put Mr. Keeler's mediumship to the acid test, and accordingly a few years since, I wrote four messages on four small slips of paper, addressed to four persons who I knew were on the "other side." I then placed them in an envelope, in the presence of a witness, sealed the flap with a special seal that I had made for the purpose, and the wax itself being of a very distinctive kind. My witness wrote his name on the flap of the envelope and we then both made affidavit before a Notary Public of this city, stating just what we had done and what was in the envelope. At the next opportunity I had of sitting with Mr. Keeler I produced this envelope and wrote a special message to his guide who claims to be George Christy, asking him as a special favor to answer the questions in the envelope.

On this occasion, however, Mr. Keeler wrote a message in pencil on one of his slates to the effect that it was not possible at this time to make the test. I may mention that Mr. Keeler did not touch the envelope at this, or at any subsequent sitting.

Several months elapsed before I had another sitting with Mr. Keeler, when I again placed the envelope on the table, hoping that the test asked for would be made. I also asked Mr. Keeler to find out if George Christy could tell me how many pieces of paper were in the envelope, and the names of those to whom they were addressed, as by this time I had really forgotten to whom I had written. After a few minutes interval Mr. Keeler picked up pencil and wrote on the slate the names of four persons whose names were on my questions, and that they were four in number. He also wrote that I was to put the envelope back in my pocket, and for the moment I was disappointed as I imagined that this meant that I was not going to get the test after all. Mr. Keeler then again used his pencil, stating that the messages had been written on in the envelope in my pocket. Mr.

Keeler showed an intense interest in this message, and urged me to open the envelope up then and there, but I refused to do so, stating that I would have it opened up before myself and a good witness, having in mind the late Dr. Walter Franklin Prince. I then wrote Dr. Prince giving him all the above facts and asking him to meet me by appointment at the Biltmore Hotel, New York, when we could open up the envelope together.

I met Dr. Prince and he examined the envelope carefully and minutely, and admitted to me that it was still sealed and bore no evidence of having been tampered with. He opened the envelope by slitting one end of it with a knife, when out came four pieces of paper addressed to the very parties whose names I had given him in advance and the answers given were pertinent to the questions asked. I then had Dr. Prince write me a letter which is in my possession now, together with the sealed envelope and the messages, in which he states positively that the envelope as handed to him was sealed.

I might add that Mr. Keeler, not knowing that I was a "researcher," allowed me perhaps special privileges, letting me handle the cards and slates myself without any aid from him.

I may also mention that the replies to my questions on the slips in the envelope were in three colors, blue, red and black, yet I am satisfied there were no colored pencils or crayons near us. I would also instance the fact that I kept the envelope in a sealed box in my residence between the time when I first produced it on Mr. Keeler's table and the time when I showed it to Mr. Prince in New York.

Sincerely yours,

Roy Holmyard.

PART II

FURTHER CORROBORATIVE EVIDENCE

THE following statements from friends I have been permitted to quote. Many other friends have received quite as good evidence.

C. R.'S EXPERIENCES WITH MR. KEELER

"Hugh Wilson was a great friend, who was killed in France during the war. In May, 1933, I had the following message from him:

" 'Dear C—— With the interest, and affection of the past I come to you today and bring you assurance of the life beyond the markings of the grave. I have been through a vast change yet I retain my personality, my individuality. It is truly a blessed privilege to meet you in this positive way. I hope you can realize my presence. I am

" 'HUGH WILSON.' "

"This message seemed to me very telling as I had wondered in previous communications whether he was the same person characteristically whom I had known. About a year later I had another message from him, as follows:

" 'You shall be cared for. Do not worry over anything. Worry kills more people than wars. I send love to all.'

"In view of his ending with the allusion to wars, seemed to me significant.

"In 1933 when I planned to have a slate writing experience with Mr. Keeler, a German friend asked me to try to get a message from a friend of hers who had passed some years previously, and whose name was Anna Helwig. I had been sitting with Mr. Keeler a few minutes when he suddenly said, 'I hear a name that sounds rather foreign. Is it Hedwig?' Later, when the cards were taken from between the slates, one of them was filled with very neat small writing from Anna Helwig. I do not recall the message, and no longer have the card, as I gave it to my friend. However, a year later I had a very wonderful message from her again, although I had *not* included her in the list of persons from whom I wished to hear. The message ran as follows:

" 'It was so. I had desired to depart,
And 'twas so when the summons were given,
There was a flutter, a pause of the heart,
A vision of angels—then heaven!'

" 'However greatly we suffer in our last illness, at the ending moments there comes a respite from all pain, and the calm of angel presences soothes us. And we never know when the change occurs. We may anticipate death, be conscious of its close approach but we do not know of the supreme change. It is like passing into sleep. You feel sleepy but never know the moment you fall into slumber. And you do not know you have slept until you awake.

" 'Always, ANNA HELWIG.'

"During the 1933 sitting I had asked for a young man who had taken his own life, whose name was Gilbert Mitchell. I no longer have this message, as I sent it to his aunt who had been very much attached to him. I only met him once, in New York, in a tall building, and I recall having been very much impressed with his message which identified him. It was about as follows:

" 'Hello C—— This is not like the sky-scraper in which we first met.'

FURTHER CORROBORATIVE EVIDENCE

"Mr. Keeler's Washington sittings are held in the two-story house, belonging to the late William Keeler.

"Again, in the sitting a year later, although I did not ask for nor did I even think of Gilbert Mitchell, he sent me the following message:

" 'If I can do something for you, call me to you, day or night. I am in the third sphere. The spirit never dies but soars upward and onward.' "

MISS MOONEY'S EXPERIENCES WITH MR. KEELER

"At Lily Dale, N. Y., in August, 1926, I had a sitting with Mr. Keeler. My mother wrote to me on that occasion. Let me state here that my mother had passed on some years before. At my home in Philadelphia I had in my possession a book in which Mother had written many times during her lifetime. Whenever she came across a bit of poetry which struck her fancy, she wrote it down. Upon returning home we compared the writing, and there was great similarity. Several letters were exactly like those made in that book by Mother some years before.

"During April and May, 1934, I again had sittings with Mr. Keeler in Washington, D. C., on three different occasions. Again Mother came and wrote. The writing was the same as that which came through at Lily Dale, eight years before.

"Mary Mooney,
"Philadelphia, Pa."

Some of Miss Mooney's messages follow:

"Dear Mary—Each time I come to you in a pronounced manifestation like this, and see others in other places doing likewise, I wonder that at least nine-tenths of the people of the mortal world are not quickly brought to a realization of the fact of life beyond the grave. It is amazing to see the lack of comprehension and understanding. The crude saying of a fact having to be knocked by a club into some people's brains, is not amiss. It takes the loss of some dearly beloved one close in rapport, the snatching of them by cruel death to force them to a thought of something after physical decease. Verily these lines of an able writer, certainly depict such a necessity:

" 'There come storms in summer weather
Lest the noontide shine too bright
There are branches in their greenness
Broken off to give us light.'

"The storm and the broken branch by death, seem necessary to stir some people into a realization of something beyond frivolity and reckless disregard.
"Devoted Mother
"Elizabeth Mooney.
"Did you tell Ruth I came?"

(Ruth—a sister in Philadelphia.)

The fine writing on this card was much like beautiful engraving. It was all contained on one side of a card 5 x 7 inches.

Wording of a card written by a relative of Miss Mooney.

"My, my but this is superlatively great. I wouldn't miss this for anything. I want my friends to know I live and enjoy life, and I shall not soon have to give it up. One death in a lifetime is enough.
"Wm. B. Lyon"
"Bill."

In the sitting Miss Mooney had on April 13th she received a message from the mother of a friend living in Philadelphia. She sent the card on to her friend, and this is her acknowledgment:

"My dear Mary—Did you do something lovely for me? My, oh! my, nothing could ever be treasured more than that writing will be. I cried and laughed together, I was so excited. I did not know how to express myself. Tuesday April 3rd Mrs. Dunlap said to me, 'You are to receive a great demonstration of mediumship in a week or two.' Of course I thought it would be here in the house, but this writing is without doubt my proof of the demonstration. Mary if you had ever seen my mother sign her name, as I have done, you would think Mama signed that note in life, and one of her sayings was, 'Don't say a word.' All the way through you can see the resemblance to Mama's writing, but the signature is perfect. Mary dear, I do not know how to thank you for even having me in mind, let alone sending me this sacred writing—it is sacred to me.
(April 19" 1934) LILLIAN."

Mrs. Dunlap mentioned is an amateur medium. Miss Mooney was not familiar with the writing.

Miss Mooney has allowed me to give parts of some of the messages which she received from Miss Ridley. In these messages were references to personal matters, of which Mr. Keeler could not have had the least information.

"I hope you had Mrs. Fletcher know that I came to you one day the first of this month. I guess it was about May 4th— You see I can count can't I. Of course I knew much about spirit return etc. but with all that, I had the old mortal love imbued in me, and I did not want to come over the river, while I was yet a young woman. It was very natural for one to cling to mortal environments, however irksome they may really be. But now that I am across the Jordan, I have no regrets about it and wouldn't resume mortal life if I could."

Another message:

"This is truly the home of the brave and the land of the free, if I have quoted that correctly. I have met many I know over here, and it is one of the most interesting of experiences to be looking every day to see who comes across the border line from the mortal side. I am truly happy."

(Very typical—she loved to watch the arrivals at Lily Dale.)

Out of several messages, Mrs. C. gave me this one, received from her mother-in-law:

"Well, how remarkable that I can be here close at your side and you not see me. But that is owing to the swift vibrations of the spirit, and the slower motion of the mortal eye. The spirit is lost to the vision of the slow moving mortal eye. The solid spokes in swiftly moving wheels are lost to the slow moving mortal eye.
"I am E—— C——."

This friend has written:

"I am glad to hear of your successful sitting with Keeler. At our last Cincinnati Psychical Research meeting (1934) until fall, Mr. Holmyard lectured on Keeler and showed us dozens of cards with messages on them."

REPORT OF MRS. W. J.

"One day my husband and I called at the home of Mr. Keeler and I went on upstairs for a 'sitting,' leaving my husband to wait downstairs.

"I had with me a paper of prepared questions rolled into a tight pellet and I personally placed this under the rubber band that held the slates together, according to the Keeler method for obtaining messages. Mr. Keeler and I sat and talked casually in the bright daylight and it seemed only a few moments before he picked up a slate pencil and wrote on top of the slates a man's name, and then a moment later he wrote 'husband' after it. He and I were entire strangers and he looked at me in surprise and said, 'Why, I supposed that was your husband who came with you!' (He had written the name of my first and deceased husband on the slate.) Later, between fragments of conversation, he wrote the names of two other friends on my list and referred conversationally to a couple of questions I had written, and all the while my little paper pellet lay in plain sight fastened on top of the slates with the rubber band.

"After about twenty minutes a tap sounded, we each held one end of the slates and the writing began. I listened and could hear the scratching between the slates. This took about four minutes and then we opened the slates and took the cards out. Before Mr. Keeler had placed the cards between the slates I had examined them to see that they were blank. Now they contained messages bearing the names of six of the seven deceased friends to whom I had written.

"About two weeks later my husband went to Mr. Keeler for a sitting and I waited downstairs as he had waited for me. My husband followed the usual procedure of putting his tightly folded paper of questions under the rubber band about the slates, but he had come with a test question, also, which his students had addressed privately to his deceased father and they had asked him to keep this in his pocket. This was to discover whether or not telepathy played any part, as my husband was ignorant of the nature of the question. However, the question he himself had asked his father on his own paper was: 'Will you answer the question in my vest pocket prepared by my class?' This test may have been said to fail because a few moments after the sitting began Mr. Keeler quite surprised my husband by saying, 'Your father says for you to take that question out of your pocket and put it on the slate.' The question in his pocket asked, 'Where and when was (your son) born? What was one peculiar circumstance at this time?' (Those familiar with psychic work will, of course, agree that this was not a particularly good type of question.) When the cards were taken out of the slates the answer was, 'I am unable to read your message all folded as it is.'

"My husband received messages from all of the seven names to which he had addressed questions.

"There are some interesting observations to be drawn from the thirteen messages he and I together received. With one exception, I cannot say that these messages are particularly evidential in context, beautiful and characteristic though they are. One, however, in its allusion to a marriage of striking interest to the parties concerned, and which was not mentioned in the question, was very evidential. But regarding the others, if one had deliberately read our questions one *could* have devised similar answers, except that in two cases of persons having unusually strong personalities, these personalities were very apparent in the messages. The handwriting of none of the people represented is similar but in two different cases where my husband and I received messages from the same persons, the handwriting of these persons is identical. If it were fraudulent, how could Mr. Keeler remember to make it the same in these instances? And in two cases the signatures are near enough like the person's own writing to have been copied. It is very amazing!

"My husband and I each received a message from a famous scientist, a friend who, in life, had done some exploring into the psychic. It is an interesting fact that many years ago this man had, himself, gone to Mr. Keeler a number of times. He had received very remarkable messages, and to satisfy his searching type of

FURTHER CORROBORATIVE EVIDENCE 33

mind had often taken a friend with him who remained in another room and watched for any evidence of trickery. But, even with an ally, this scientist was unable to discover any indications of fraud.

"C. J."

FROM MISS M. BELLE CROSS

"My first experience with Mr. Keeler was at Lily Dale in August, 1926.

"I went as one of the many hundreds of others there, who were unknown and most unknowing—many expecting to see some mysterious, dim chamber, with weird rites performed, or else a rabbit jump out of a hat! But all who came and went saw just the same big sunny open room, with a handsome, kindly-faced, gray-haired man, seated at a window opening out on the sparkling lake. I had written seven questions on a small sheet of ordinary size letter paper, then folded it closely and rolled it into a tiny spill. This was in my pocket and in my hand all the time, until slipped under the rubber bands holding together the two slates, and then held firmly under my finger—never unloosed from under my thumb. After about ten minutes of commonplace conversation, we got the familiar 'tap' under the slates. Both Mr. Keeler and I lifted the slates, and held by opposite ends. I looked at my watch. In one minute and twenty seconds, during which we heard the furious sound of writing inside the slates—came another tap. Mr. Keeler released his hold, and left me to open the slates. The first card was signed by the name first on my question list, a close relative, and in such unmistakable similarity to the communicator's life signature, H. C. V. Campbell, which I found two months later on old bank vouchers, that several cashiers told me the card signature would be accepted by any bank—but that was not all. The message began:

" 'When we stand by the bed of a passing friend and

note the fluttering breath and feeble pulse, we feel that this must truly be the *end* of life. Not so, it is on the death bed that real life begins; it is only the earth life that is unreal.'

"The crux of this message was that fifteen years before I stood *alone* by the bedside of this good man and dear relative, hand on pulse and felt its last beat, in a little unknown West Virginia town. All the other cards held personality and evidence equally convincing.

"This little incident may be of interest to many:

"I had a sitting with Mr. Keeler soon after the passing of Harry Houdini, and had placed his name on my list. The required number of cards were put between the slates and one came out a blank. When I called Mr. Keeler's attention to it, he quietly replied, 'My Guides would not let him come in.' I wonder was it because he was still a 'Trickster' in death, as well as in life?

"The following year I was again at Lily Dale. Mr. Keeler did not remember me, but I was given a date. We sat under the same conditions except the day was damp and cloudy. After thirty minutes' waiting we gave up; nothing at all, no sign of life came about the slates. I should like to say that Mr. Keeler never charges a cent when there is a failure. Later on I secured another date on a fine day and had equally good results as the first time.

"For the next date with Mr. Keeler, at Lily Dale, I wrote in my room, two lists of names, each different— no duplication. Each piece of paper the same kind, folded the same, and each placed in the same type of envelope and sealed. These were placed in a locked drawer, where they remained for two weeks, before I had the date with Mr. Keeler. Meanwhile I had forgotten what the names were on the two separate lists. So I took one of the envelopes, still sealed, in my pocket (where it remained) to the sitting. That time our waiting was twenty minutes, but there was reward. The cards had messages from three on the list with me, and there were messages from five on the list I had left in my own room, sealed, and two extra ones not on either list, meant for friends in Baltimore.

"Many cases of extra or unsought messages come from strangers trying to get loving words over our telephone or radio, to dear ones whom we might find for them.

"After my 1927 sitting for Mrs. Fletcher several years passed, and my next contact with Mr. Keeler was in Washington, D. C.—February 20th, 1933. Mrs. Fletcher and I went together for sittings. I wrote my list of questions at home the day before, and placed them by my mother's picture. There were eight names on this list—one name belonging to a dear friend, of an acquaintance in Washington, who desired to hear from this man. I also wrote the name of this man and the name of my physician of twenty years past, and also that of a young man who had passed on (as the result of a motor accident), on another slip of paper, sealed it, and left it in my room at Mrs. Fletcher's home. No one knew of this. I took the list of eight names with me—only one was a duplicate of one on the list at home. My time was about fifteen minutes' waiting for the signal, and less than two minutes for the finished writing. Five on my list in my hand had written good messages—two of whom had communicated in my first sitting. They referred to places and events, that had occurred during the interim. This from a fine old Confederate soldier on account of whose lameness I had often given a helping hand.

" 'Didn't you see me come in? I am glad that I can get about without crutches. Not Gen'l now.
" 'Just ED. P. ALEXANDER.'
"(Perfect life signature.)

"One on my list at home answered thus:

"'I am pleased to be one of the choice friends gathered here this morning to greet you. It is blessed that there is a link to bind the universe together. I am often near to help you.

"'D̶r. Robert T. Wilson.'

"(Dr. blue penciled out. Signature like life.)

"The boy on my list at home wrote:

"'Tell Mother I was here. I am trying to keep boys from harm, who are in such a hurry to go no-where.'

"This boy was killed in an auto smash.

"The man whose name I had duplicated never showed up at all! Where's telepathy?

"On one card were five different messages in individual and unlike writing. There were in all on the cards that day, thirteen names not asked for, anywhere, several not known to me personally.

"The last card was a most charming valentine of verse and flowers in exquisite drawing. Several artists have told me that no mortal could duplicate such work in less than an hour. This loving communicator was one who came without call—save of the heart."

PART III

TAILS FROM "THE HAPPY HUNTING GROUND"

PART III

TAILS FROM "THE HAPPY HUNTING GROUND"

WHILE on a visit to my daughter in St. Louis, in the summer of 1932, I had the privilege of attending a séance in the home of Mrs. Myrtle Larsen, the renowned trumpet medium. During some remarkable manifestations, I felt something nosing about my feet, and patting my knee. Suddenly I said, "Oh! it is a dog, is it Mutt?" "Mutt" being the last dog we had owned, I thought of him first. "No," answered Sunflower, the bright little Indian girl in Mrs. Larsen's band, "this dog's name is Bobbie; but why did you name a lady dog Bobbie?" There was not the slightest chance that any one in the circle, save my daughter and myself, knew that we once owned a little female fox terrier called "Bobbie."

Many years ago, during a first meeting with a clairvoyant medium from Philadelphia, she described "Bobbie" perfectly, and the familiar antics she was displaying about me.

The summer of 1933, I was again a member of a circle held with Mrs. Larsen, and again I felt a gentle tap, tap against my ankle as Sunflower said, "This is a little black dog, and she is hitting you with her tail." Of course it was poor little Phillie, who had become a member of the family through compassion, and whose dainty black and tan body was marred by a top-heavy tail, inherited from some obscure ancestor. She and Bobbie were great friends, and I can visualize the maneuvers that passed in Dog Heaven when Bobbie was imparting to Phillie how she could again come in contact with her "white folks."

Sunflower also said, "There is a parrot here, too, named

Lucy." Yes, there was once a parrot in the family named "Lucy."

When we returned to Washington that year, we brought with us two Silver Persian kittens. In about a month we noticed that the one we had named Felim was seemingly ill. Our first thought was that the disturbance was caused by that bane of long-haired cats, hair-balls—but the veterinary who treated him notified us that there must be something much more serious at work. An X-ray showed a round spot of metal in his stomach—an operation produced a dime, as black as ink. Peritonitis had developed with a temperature of 104°. It may seem absurd to many to send out a radio supplication mentally to someone in the Spirit World. But what else is prayer? Remembering Sunflower's interest in our pets, I sent out into the ether vibrations, as intense a call as I could command, "Sunflower, help." My daughter, meanwhile, had been hoping for the help of Dr. Parker, Mrs. Larsen's Guide.

I wrote to Mrs. Emily Grant Hutchings, of St. Louis, author of that charming book, *Where Do We Go From Here?*, telling her of the illness of our pet, and his subsequent recovery. She answered that at one of Mrs. Larsen's circles, both Dr. Parker and Sunflower had communicated. When she inquired if Dr. Parker knew anything about our cat, he replied, "Ask Sunflower." Then Sunflower explained how the cat had managed to swallow the dime—and said, "Dr. Parker might think it was beneath his dignity to minister to a cat, but he did it just the same—he would have died if Dr. Parker had not helped with the operation."

When the veterinary said that "the cat's recovery had been miraculous" he spoke truer than he knew.

On my surreptitiously pasted paper of the 1934 sitting with Mr. Keeler, I had written: "Sunflower—Are you and the Doctor still taking care of our pet?"

On one of the cards, on which were written two other messages, I found this:

> "ME STILL WATCH OVER MY SWEET CHARGE.
> SUN FLOWER"

To Miss Cross, in a sitting with Mrs. Hughes in Baltimore, my mother came, sending this message to me:

> "Tell her I have quite a few of her cats over here. I don't know her names for them, but I know she loved them, and I will keep them for her."

Once in a circle with Miss Hazel Ridley, a dear little boy, telling his parents of his life in the Spirit World, said:

> "I am just fine, Grandpa and Aunt Roxie are standing here. How is Dickie? Here is a nice colored lady—I don't know her, but she said 'That I am a nice little man.' Say, do you know there is a parrot here?"

My father said to me, through Miss Ridley:

> "Yes, there is an animal sphere with lower and higher planes, just as mortal spirits have. The love of mortals can never reach the strength of the love of our animal pets."

In one of the materialization manifestations, given by Mrs. Elizabeth Allen Tomson, in my home, a young woman among the sitters positively asserted that her little black dog had materialized.

A few months after he passed to "the happy land," the young man who gave the remarkable demonstration of the dog sketch on the Keeler card, came through Miss Ridley and said:

"Why, do you know you are not dead—we meet every one we know over here. That big yellow cat of yours, came to me and rubbed all about me—he knew me—I can't think of his name." "Do you mean Pinch?" I said. "Yes, that's the one," answered Charles.

If, as many attempt to prove, telepathy plays the principal part in these manifestations, why was that name obscure in the young man's memory, while it was perfectly clear in mine?

The London *Graphic* of Sunday, July 8, 1934, printed an article by Sir Oliver Lodge entitled, "How Children and Animals Live in the Next World," which has this to say in regard to animals:

> "The higher animals have developed some human qualities. They have attained a stage at which there is individual memory, which is the beginning of personality. Some of them have attained a stage at which love for their human friends is dominant. My Son tells me that his favorite dog came to welcome him, and that he and others are not cut off from their animal friends."

Swedenborg wrote:

> "The reason that nothing in nature exists but from a spiritual origin—is that there cannot be anything in existence unless it have a soul."